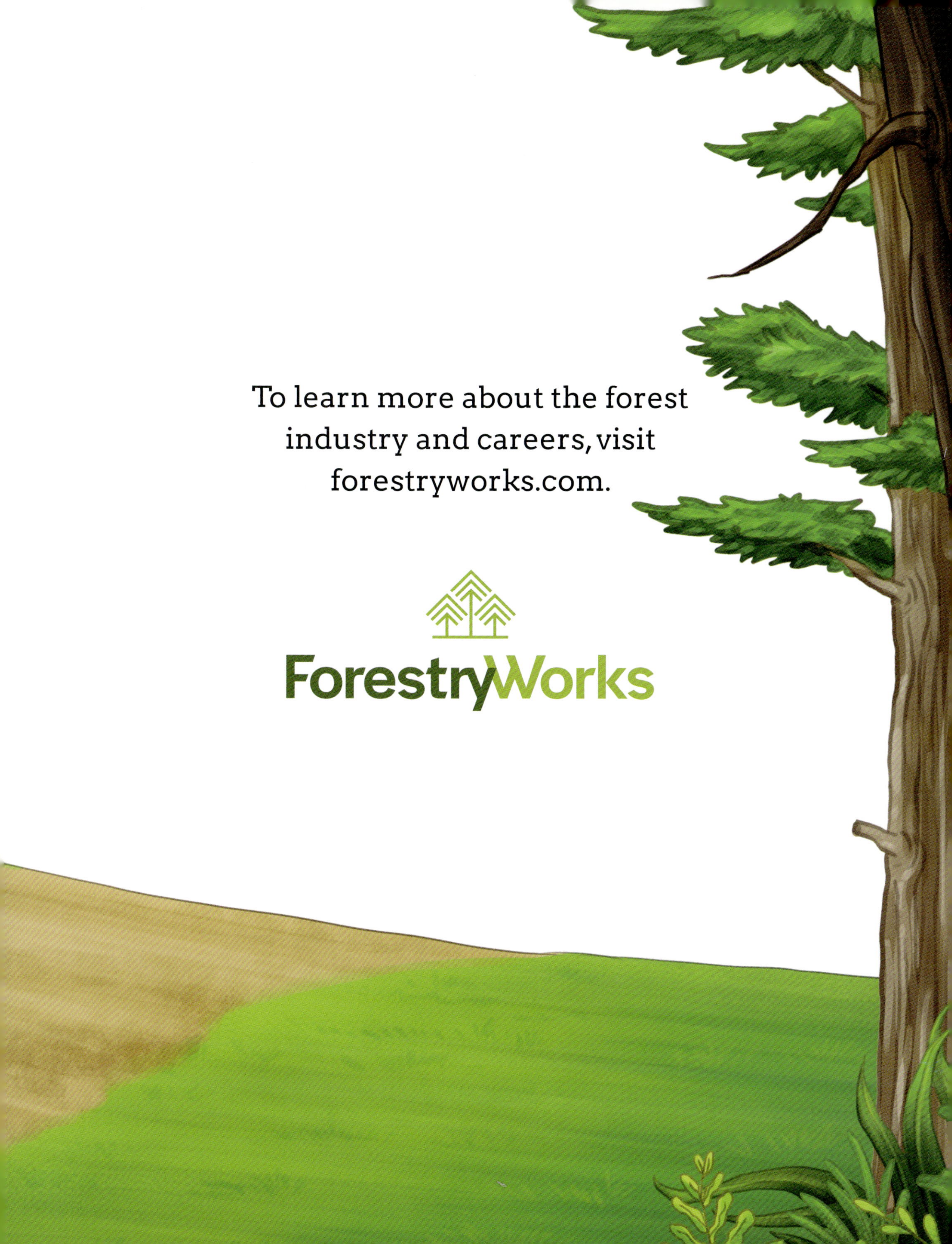
To learn more about the forest industry and careers, visit forestryworks.com.

Sam Visits a Sawmill

For more information, please contact:
Mascot Kids, an imprint of Amplify Publishing Group
620 Herndon Parkway, Suite 220
Herndon, VA 20170
info@mascotbooks.com

Library of Congress Control Number: 2023906317

CPSIA Code: PRKF0224A

ISBN-13: 978-1-63755-733-4

Printed in China

Tiny Timber Crew:
Sam
VISITS A
Sawmill
Stephanie Fuller
Illustrated by Agus Prajogo

In Sam's town there is a sawmill,
that big shiny building on the hill.

A sawmill is home to big machines
that cut logs into boards and pallets
and beams.

Sam's friend, Nick, works in the mill.
He invited her to visit. What a great deal!

Nick and Sam work out a plan to tour the mill from beginning to end.

SAUNDERS
LOGGING

Truck driver Anne delivers her logs cut from trees.
Once they're in the mill, there's so much they can be!

The logs' first stop is at the scale house to be weighed.
In a safe spot, Sam and Nick stayed.

Sam and Nick, watch out for the crane!
Waving from way up high is Operator Wayne.

Wayne's job is to unload the trucks
by using a huge claw to pick the logs up.

The logs are stacked into neat piles.
Piled so high and stacked for miles!

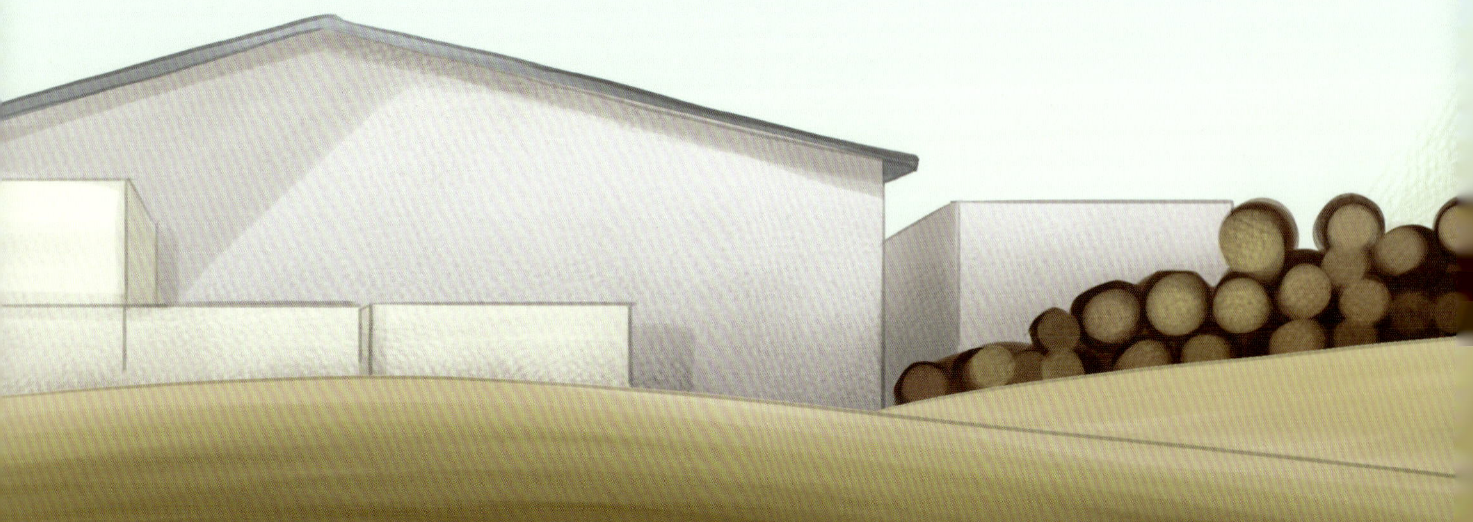

Logs from the pile go into the mill.
When they visit the debarker, they don't sit still.

The debarker removes the bark using sharp blades,
then on to the head rig to cut at the right place.

A log's bark and leftover pieces
are taken somewhere else to be used for other reasons.

The bare, short log then moves to the scanner.
It tells the saws how to cut in a neat manner.

With the merch saw, one log can make many pieces.
A *cant* is the sawed-off piece that it releases.

The next step is to cut the wood into boards, then trimmed and placed and stacked and stored.

Many people like Tom and Cat work on the line. They make sure the mill keeps running just fine!

The boards are stacked, neat and clean.
The kiln gets them dry, making all that steam!

When the boards are dry and ready to move,
they are sent to the planer mill operated by Sue.

The planer mill smooths the boards to get rid of splinters.
This makes a board ready for the packer and printer.

The packer machine, big and fast,
restacks the boards and bundles them with straps.

When Sam visits the last machine in the mill,
she meets Larry the labeler,
who labels bundles with skill.

The bundles of boards are loaded on trucks
by a speedy forklift—look, there's Chuck!

Once the lumber is loaded and secured,
it is taken to the store and could be yours!

LUMBER
LUMBER
LUMBER

Sawmills make boards and pallets and strips and beams
used to build houses and porches and playsets with swings!

All of these cool things come from trees.
And when that tree was harvested, they planted a new seed.

Sam was excited as she left the sawmill with Nick.
Sawmills are exciting, and the machines
move so quick!

There are lots of important people
who work in a sawmill.
They do a fantastic job in that
shiny building on the hill.

About the Author

Stephanie Fuller works for the Forest Workforce Training Institute. Since she grew up rooted in a logging family, it is no surprise that her passion led her to a career in forestry. Stephanie's goal for writing The Tiny Timber Crew™ series is to educate children about sustainable forestry practices and the people whose job it is to take care of our forests.

ForestryWorks® is the jobs promotion initiative of the Forest Workforce Training Institute. The mission of ForestryWorks® is to create a pipeline of workers for the forest industry through education, career promotion, and training. This pipeline will create a sustainable source of forest professionals for generations to come.

Visit forestryworks.com to learn more about jobs in the forest industry.